To Alasdair, Duncan, Lochlan, Finn,
and freedom-loving children everywhere.

And with thanks to the staff of the Minute Man National Historical Park, to David Wood, curator of the Concord Museum, and to the many historians who have researched, written, and preserved the story of the beginning of the Revolutionary War.

www.mascotbooks.com

The Other Midnight Rider: Sam Prescott Rides for Freedom

For more information, please contact:
Mascot Kids, an imprint of Amplify Publishing Group
620 Herndon Parkway, Suite 220
Herndon, VA 20170
info@mascotbooks.com

Library of Congress Control Number: 2025925026

CPSIA Code: PRF0226A

ISBN-13: 979-8-90026-039-6

Printed in Canada

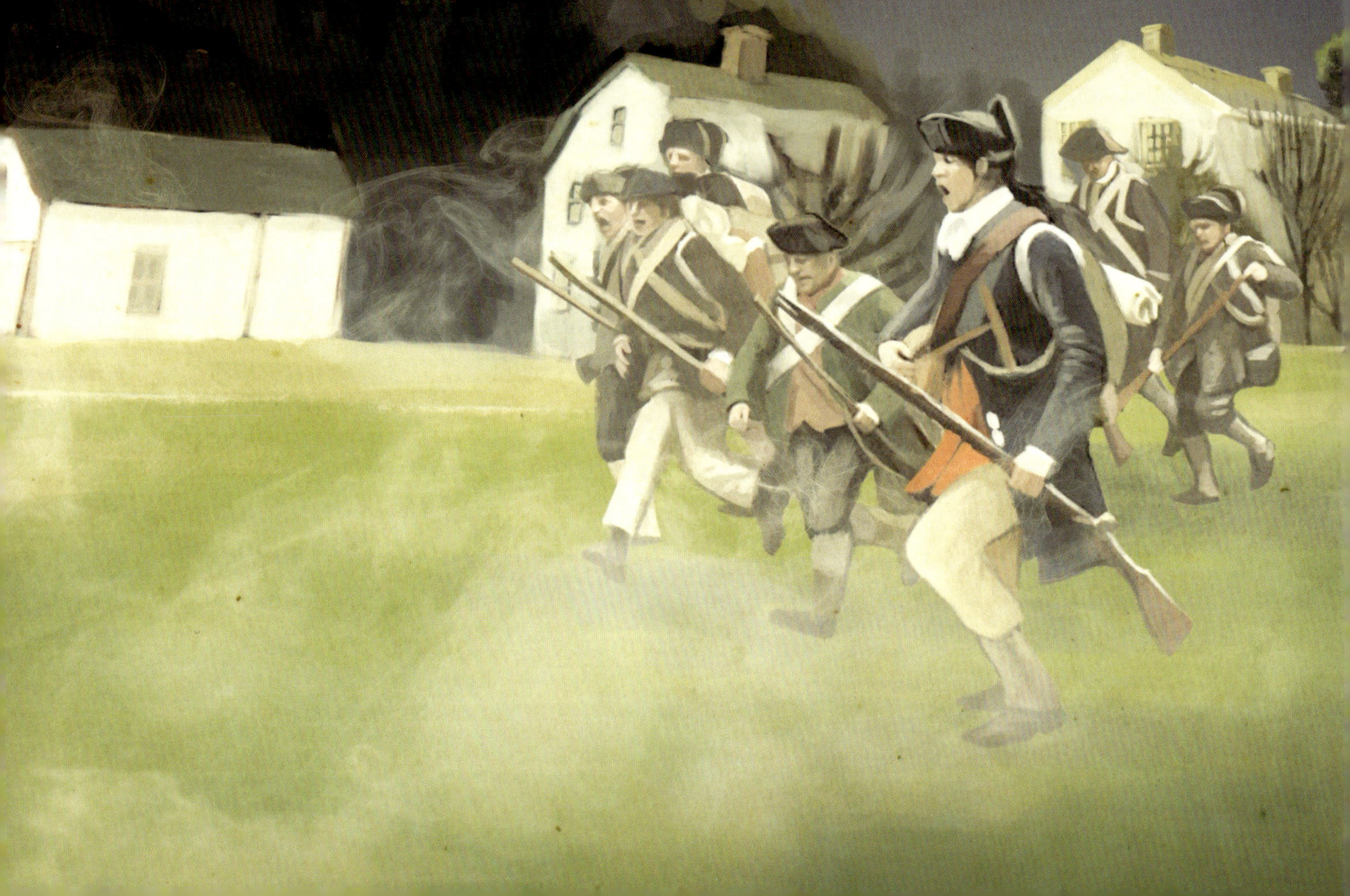

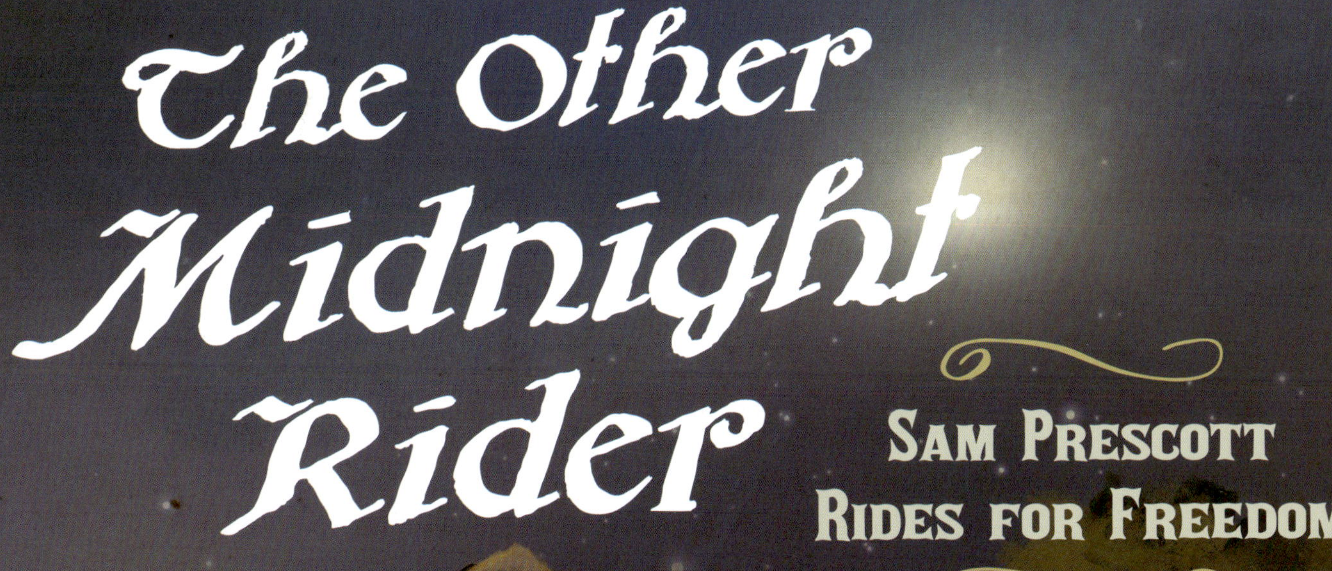

The Other Midnight Rider

Sam Prescott Rides for Freedom

Eileen Cameron

Illustrated by Marco Primo

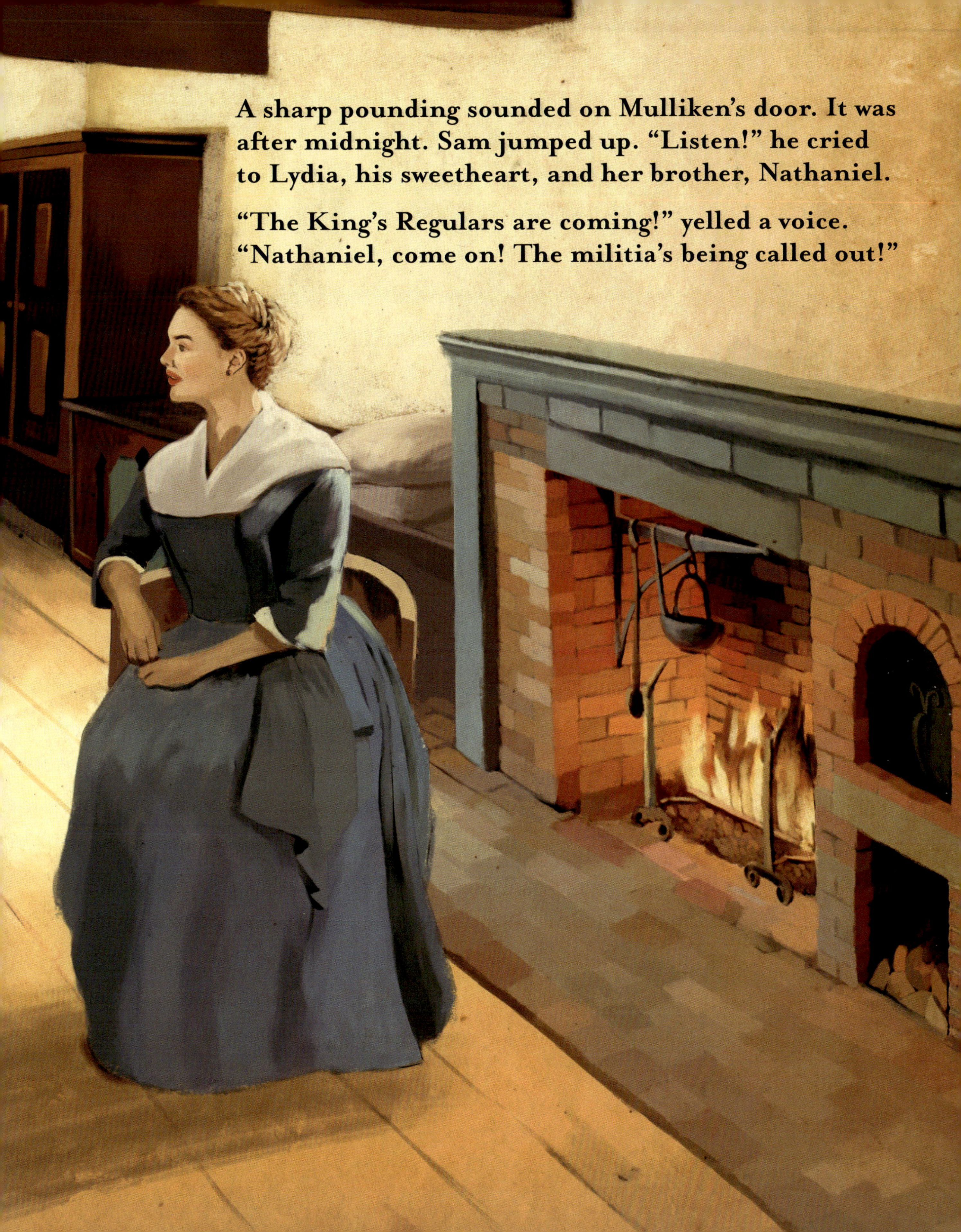

A sharp pounding sounded on Mulliken's door. It was after midnight. Sam jumped up. "Listen!" he cried to Lydia, his sweetheart, and her brother, Nathaniel.

"The King's Regulars are coming!" yelled a voice. "Nathaniel, come on! The militia's being called out!"

"The King's men are riding to grab our supplies!" gasped the militiaman. "Paul Revere, the rider from Boston, just brought the news!"

"They'll be after Sam Adams and John Hancock, the patriot leaders. They're at Reverend Clarke's home," said Nathaniel.

"And, they want our weapons in Concord!" shouted the militiaman. Nathaniel grabbed his musket and dashed out into the night.

Sam and Lydia stood stunned. They listened to the town alarm bell ring and watched lights flicker on in the nearby houses.

"Now, after all the King's unfair laws and taxes, they want to take our supplies!" said Sam. "I'd better be off for home, Lydia."

"I hope the Regulars won't come all this way from Boston," worried Lydia.

Sam swung into the saddle and called to her. "Don't worry too much, but be sure to bar the door!"

"I will!" Lydia called back. "Be careful!"

Sam galloped down the road past the Lexington Common. The town Minutemen were racing to the Green. Then, the young doctor turned down the Bay Road to Concord and home.

I hope nothing bad happens tonight with the Regulars, he thought anxiously. *We colonists might need the guns to protect ourselves.*

Nearing the hamlet of Lincoln, Sam spotted two riders ahead. He slowed for a minute. *Is this a King's patrol or Sons of Liberty?* he thought. He saw that their horses had been ridden hard.

He overtook the riders, and the first stranger said, "Sir, isn't it late to be abroad?"

"Just leaving Lexington. The town is wide awake," said Sam. "Have you heard?"

"Heard what?" asked the first rider.

"Some news was brought from Boston. Where are you gentlemen riding from?" Sam asked.

"Boston," said the second rider.

"Have you stopped in Lexington?" asked Sam.

"Yes, we visited Reverend Clarke at the parsonage," said one.

Sam relaxed. "Then you must be the alarm riders. I'm Sam Prescott, a Son of Liberty," he said.

"Paul Revere and William Dawes," said Revere. "We're carrying the alarm on to Concord so they can hide the colony's weapons for our militias."

"A lot of supplies were moved today," said Sam. "Men buried cannons in the fields and hid gunpowder in cellars. Women helped conceal the barrels of beef and rice. But a lot is still to be done. I'll ride with you. I know the roads and people."

The three men galloped hard down the road. Sam and Dawes slowed to warn a cluster of houses, calling, "Wake up! The Regulars are coming!" Revere sped on down the road.

Suddenly, Sam saw two horsemen pull out of the shadows up ahead and rush Revere.

"Move up, men! Let's ride through them!" called Revere. Sam and Dawes dug in their heels and raced toward Revere. More horsemen darted out of the trees.

"Stop!" they barked. "Stop!"

One yelled, "If you go an inch further, you are a dead man!" *A King's patrol!* Sam stared. The three patriots urged their horses on and tried to drive through the soldiers. They were outnumbered. The soldiers pointed their guns at the patriots and drove them toward a pasture.

A trap! Sam looked around, heart racing, searching for an escape route. He whispered to Revere, "Put on! Let's go! Go!"

Sam broke off fast, wielded his horse to the left, shot through the pasture, and jumped the stone wall. Revere veered to the right, looking for another way out of the field.

"Halt!" commanded the Regulars. They circled Revere and grabbed him. Dawes, seeing his chance, turned and hurtled back down the road toward Lexington and into the night.

Sam looked back. *I can't believe they've got Revere,* he thought. *And Dawes is gone! I must get to Concord on my own. I must get through!* He raced through the woods and plunged down a slope. Tree limbs smacked at his legs, and pine boughs stung his face. His horse stumbled, almost pitching him off as he plowed through the dark undergrowth.

He peered into the darkness, searching for a familiar path. He slowed through a low marsh and paused. Heart beating, he listened for the sound of pursuing Regulars.

He finally found the Bay Road near Hartwell's tavern. "The Regulars are coming! Sound the alarm for the Lincoln Minutemen!" he cried. Then he cautiously peered out on the road. No Regulars in sight. He raced out into the moonlight.

Ride! he told himself urgently. *Ride! It's up to you to warn Concord!* Sam pressed on and pushed full tilt down the hill and past the meadows. He pounded past sleeping houses, shouting, "The Regulars are coming!"

He thundered into Concord. It was the early hours of the morning. “The alarm!” he shouted to the night watch at the town meeting house. “The Regulars are out! Sound the alarm!” The sentry yanked the bell rope, and the alarm clanged, loud in the quiet night.

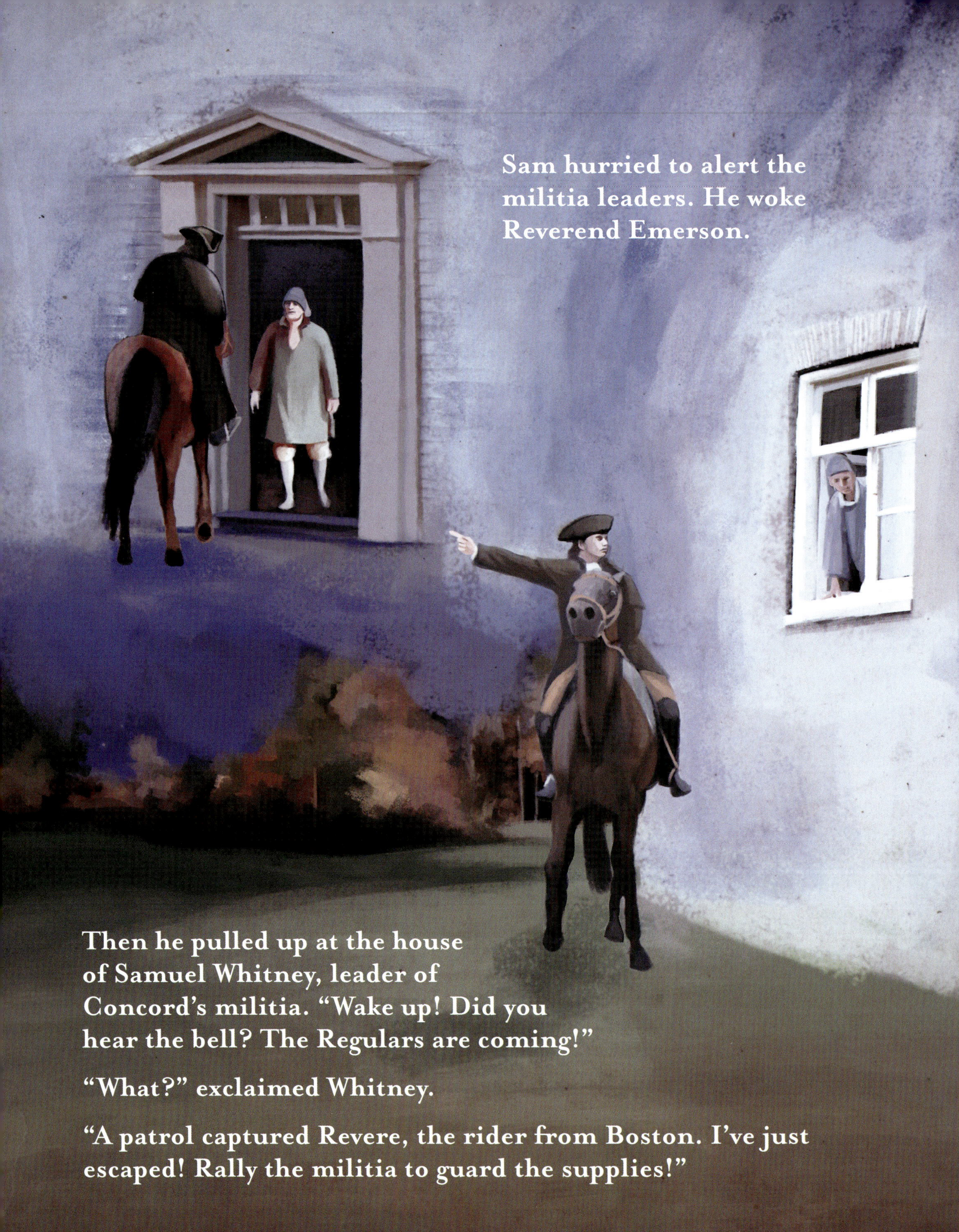

Sam hurried to alert the militia leaders. He woke Reverend Emerson.

Then he pulled up at the house of Samuel Whitney, leader of Concord's militia. "Wake up! Did you hear the bell? The Regulars are coming!"

"What?" exclaimed Whitney.

"A patrol captured Revere, the rider from Boston. I've just escaped! Rally the militia to guard the supplies!"

Sam turned and sprinted to his own home, shouting for his brother. "Up, Abel! Wake up!"

"The Regulars are on the way to steal our supplies. I'm riding to Acton to warn them! Will you take the southern route?"

"Yes! I'll take the towns of Sudbury and Framingham," called Abel, as he mounted his horse and sped out of the yard after Sam.

As Sam raced on to Acton, he saw that Concord had awakened. Militiamen rushed in from all directions. Sam felt a surge of pride. "We colonists are willing to fight for our rights and liberties! Now, I must get through to Acton!"

Author's Note

In the early hours of April 19, 1775, Sam Prescott succeeded in getting the news to Concord that the Regulars of the British Army were riding to surprise the colonists and seize their weapons.

As Sam rode on to alarm Acton, the Lexington militia had gathered on the town Common. As the early sun rose, they saw the large contingent of Regulars appear on the road from Boston. Captain John Parker, militia leader, cautioned the men assembled on the Common: "Hold your fire. Don't fire first."

But a shot was fired, by which side is unknown, and soldiers opened fire against each other. In a short time, eight Lexington men lay dead and a number were wounded. The Regulars had one soldier wounded. The Regulars then marched on to Concord.

During the day, close to 4,000 militiamen, alerted by Revere, Dawes, Prescott, and many other riders who had fanned out across the state, arrived in Concord. Approximately 400 militiamen defended the Concord Bridge against the British troops. Here, the American colonists took their stand for the second time in the day against the 1,500 men of the British army, saving some of their supplies.

The Regulars retreated for the nearly twenty-mile hike back to Boston as the growing militia pursued them, taking shots from behind walls and trees. The American Revolution had begun. The Massachusetts militiamen had defended their rights as Englishmen. If the King and Parliament wouldn't grant them their liberties, they would fight for a new and free country.

Within days, 20,000 militiamen from around New England joined the Massachusetts units and aided in the siege of the British in Boston. When word spread to the other colonies, men rushed to join their colony's militia. Many supported the Massachusetts militias barricading the King's forces in Boston.

The Continental Congress, representatives from the thirteen colonies, which was meeting in Philadelphia, commissioned the Continental Army and appointed General George Washington of Virginia to be Commander on June 15, 1775. The American Revolutionary War was on and would last for eight long years.

As Sam Prescott rode to alert Acton in the early hours of April 19, 1775, he could not have imagined that what he and the other Midnight Riders had done on this spring night and early morning would help create a great free and independent nation.

THE HEROES OF THE NIGHT

Dr. Sam Prescott

Sam was the only alarm rider to reach Concord in the early morning hours of April 19, 1775. He helped save the colonists' supplies as the first battle of the American Revolutionary War took place. His story after that night in 1775 is largely unknown, but there are reports that list a Dr. Prescott as a surgeon at Fort Ticonderoga in 1776. Years later, a Revolutionary War veteran reported in his memoirs that there had been a Prescott with him in the British prison in Halifax in 1777. It is widely believed that Sam Prescott died in the Halifax prison. He was twenty-six years old.

Lydia Mulliken

According to traditional stories, Lydia waited for the duration of the war for her fiancé, Sam, to return. Some years after the end of the war, Lydia married another gentleman. The stories tell the tale of the romance between Dr. Prescott and Lydia, but there are no confirmed reports of this. Dr. Prescott may have been visiting a sick patient the night of April 18-19, 1775, when he met Revere and Dawes on the Concord Road.

Abel Prescott

Young Abel Prescott was shot by a Regular soldier on his return ride from Sudbury the morning of April 19, 1775, and died of his wounds several months later.

Nathaniel Mulliken

Nathaniel, Lydia's brother and the town clockmaker, served with the local Lexington militia and died six months after the April 19th ride, possibly of camp fever. He was twenty-three.

William Dawes

Dawes, a professional tanner from Boston, fell from his horse that fateful night and walked back to Lexington. During the Revolutionary War, he served in a Boston regiment as a quartermaster. After the war, he resumed his flourishing trade. He died at age fifty-three. His descendants include several US congressmen and a vice president of the United States.

Paul Revere

Revere, a well-known silversmith from Boston, served as an officer in the Massachusetts militia during the Revolutionary War. Following the war, he continued his silversmithing, and as technology changed, he expanded into iron casting and copper forging, becoming experienced in the new industries. He lived a long life, dying at age eighty-three. He had many grandchildren. His descendants include his grandson, who was a Union Army general in the Civil War, and many successful entrepreneurs. He lived to see a great new nation grow and prosper into a thriving democratic republic.

The Minutemen

Once the alarm was received, many courageous men of the local militias, men who vowed to be ready in a minute, took up arms and raced to Concord and Lexington to protect their supplies and liberties. They walked and rode from towns and hamlets across the state. They continued to spread the alarm to local towns and to the other American colonies.

Reverend William Emerson

Dr. Emerson was the pastor of the Concord First Parish Church. He, as did many New England ministers, preached that men and women had the right to their own consciences, choices, and speech. He spoke against British tyranny and called for the people's right to liberty as "their birthright as Englishmen." Dr. Emerson joined the Continental Army as a chaplain. On his way home from service in Fort Ticonderoga in 1776, he became ill and died. He was thirty-three. His grandson was Ralph Waldo Emerson.

ABOUT THE AUTHOR

Eileen Cameron is a celebrated children's author and historic preservationist who holds degrees from Skidmore College and NYU. Her book *Canyon*, was a Bank Street College's Book of the Year; *G is for Garden State* was named Book of the Year by the New Jersey Center for the Book; and *Rupert's Parchment: Story of Magna Carta* was featured at Magna Carta Day at the National Archives in Washington, DC, and was a Foreword Reviews Picture Book/Early Reader Book of Year Finalist.

She has served on the Life Guard Society Board at George Washington's Mount Vernon and on the board of the Washington Association of New Jersey. Visit her website at eileencameron.com.